William J. Chalmers Masters

The Rose of Salency

An Operetta

William J. Chalmers Masters

The Rose of Salency
An Operetta

ISBN/EAN: 9783337320591

Hergestellt in Europa, USA, Kanada, Australien, Japan

Cover: Foto ©Thomas Meinert / pixelio.de

Weitere Bücher finden Sie auf **www.hansebooks.com**

The
ROSE OF SALENCY,
An Operetta,

WRITTEN AND COMPOSED
BY
W. CHALMERS MASTERS.

ENT. STA. HALL.   PRICE 15/.

LONDON,
LAMBORN COCK, HUTCHINGS & Cᵒ (late LEADER & COCK) 62 & 63, NEW BOND STREET.

This Work consists of an OVERTURE, DANCE, & FIFTEEN VOCAL PIECES.
all of which may be had separately.

LIBRETTOS SIXPENCE EACH.
ALL APPLICATIONS RESPECTING THE LIBRETTO OF THIS WORK, TO BE MADE TO THE PUBLISHERS.
62 & 63, NEW BOND STREET.

The Composer reserves to himself the right of Publication of this Work; in all Foreign Countries.

To

M. W. BALFE. ESQ^{RE}.

This Operetta

Is Dedicated

(with permission)

By his Obliged Friend

W. CHALMERS MASTERS.

January, 1863.

THE ROSE OF SALENCY.
AN OPERETTA.

WORDS AND MUSIC BY W. CHALMERS MASTERS.

CHARACTERS.

*CAPTAIN ANTOINE, Son of the Seigneur of the Village ....Tenor.

The PASTOR of the Village....Bass.   *PIERRE, a Soldier—brother to Lisette ....Tenor.

LISETTE, a Village Maiden.............Soprano.   THÉRÈSE, a Villager ....Mezzo Soprano.

*In the absence of Two Tenors these parts can be taken by one.

ACT I.

SCENE I.—*The Village Street. Lisette's Cottage on one side. Near a large tree a table is placed, with an urn on it.*

CHORUS.

Upon this day we meet to choose
A maiden for our village Queen;
On her alone our choice shall fall
Whose life has pure and spotless been.
Nor wit nor beauty shall decide,
But virtue be our only guide.

PASTOR. Now, neighbours all, each in your turn,
Pass by, and place within this urn
The paper with the maiden's name
Whom you would wish o'er you to reign,
And till another year comes round,
To be your Queen with roses crown'd.

CHORUS.

Now hope and fear are striving
In many a maiden's breast,
But soon their fate deciding,
Each doubt will be at rest.
We think the maiden we can see
Whom all would wish their Queen to be.

PAS. My friends, with pleasure I announce to all,
Upon Lisette your choice doth fall.

CHORUS.

Happy Lisette, rejoice!
On thee hath fall'n our choice;
And happy are we to gain
Such a Queen o'er us to reign.
Thy pure and spotless mind,
Thy beauty and truth combin'd,
Will make us all hail the day
When we bow to thy gentle sway.

SONG.—LISETTE.

I.

O happy day! what joy to know
I shall be Queen of Roses!
What bliss to feel that on my brow
The beauteous wreath reposes!
What transport my dear friends to meet—
Each cheek with pleasure glowing;
And all a smile, and welcome kind,
Upon their Queen bestowing!

II.

When lads and lasses, gaily dressed,
Are on the green sward dancing,
And from each maiden's sparkling eye
Pure happiness is glancing—
When Music's notes float in the air,
Mine ear with welcome greeting—
Believe me, friends, this heart will then
With gratitude be beating.

PAS. At church to-morrow we will meet,
Each one drest
All in his best,
And there our future Queen we'll greet.
Then 'neath the sacred dome we'll pray
That Heaven will guide her on her way,
And shield her from all care and sorrow.—
So now farewell until to-morrow.

CHORUS.

Till the sun the orient sky
Is tinting with golden ray,
And nature wakes, rejoicing
To welcome another day:
Till, through the ambient air,
Is heard the matin bell,
Farewell, fair Queen of Roses,—
Gentle Lisette, farewell.

LIS. Farewell, dear friends and neighbours,
Until the morn, farewell.
[*Exeunt all. Lisette enters her cottage.*]

SCENE II.—*Interior of Lisette's cottage; an image of the Virgin against the wall. Lisette enters.*

LIS. O this has been a happy day!
How kind my neighbours were that they

Should choose the orphan-girl Lisette
To be their Queen of Roses—yet
I cannot help a feeling of regret
My brother is not here to share
My joy. Now I'll to rest repair—
But first I'll offer up a prayer.

I.

O Holy Virgin guard
Thy servant thro' the night;
And o'er her slumbers watch
Until the morning light.

II.

While darkness shrouds the earth
From danger keep me free;
And in the morn I'll sing
Glad praises unto thee.
[*She lights a candle, and is about to retire.*]

LIS. What step is that? Who comes this way?
[*Enter Pierre.*]

My brother Pierre!

PIERRE. Hush! silence, pray!
Are we alone? Is no one near?

LIS. We are alone. But why this fear?
Why on that face that look forlorn,
Thy dress all travel-stained and torn?—
What means all this?

PIERRE. My tongue will fail
To tell thee all the dreadful tale.

BALLAD.—PIERRE.

I.

Thou know'st that I was forced to leave
This happy, humble cot,
To join the busy tented field,
And share a soldier's lot;
But 'midst the din and clang of arms,
In battle's fierce array,
I thought of thee, my sister dear,
And the cottage far away.

II.

At night I paced the sentry's round,
To guard against surprise;
I gazed upon the starry heavens,
And thought of thy bright eyes.
'Midst all the scenes of war and strife
For one thing did I pray—
Once more to see my sister dear
And the cottage far away.

LIS. Keep me no longer in suspense, dear Pierre;
Tell me what dire misfortune brings you here.

PIERRE. Thou know'st, Lisette, our Seigneur's son
By valiant deeds has honor won;
But tho' a soldier brave is he,
He laughs at woman's purity.
One day he dared to join thy name
With words of infamy and shame:
Enraged, I struck him—swords we drew—
We fought—alas! my sword plunged thro'
His side—he fell, and lay as dead;
Struck with remorse and fear I fled,
For days and nights I wandered on,
Till tired and worn, all hope near gone,
I reached, at last, this much-loved home.
(*Aside.*) Should I be found, death is my doom.

DUET.

As when the threat'ning thunder-cloud
Obscures the summer light,
And over hill and valley casts
A shadow as of night:
So now I feel that sorrow's blight
Has fall'n upon the scene,
And grief usurps the place where once
Reign'd happiness supreme.

LISETTE.

Hark! I hear footsteps in the street,
The neighbours near my window meet.
Quick, to my bedroom—take this light;
All angels guard thee, Pierre—Good night!
[*Pierre takes the candle, and enters Lisette's bedroom. Lisette falls on her knees before the image of the Virgin.*]

SERENADE *(outside)*

Sweet dreams attend thy sleeping,
    Maiden fair,
All angels o'er thee keeping
    Watchful care,
Until the lark is singing
    His matin lay,
And village bells are ringing
    In the day.
Sweet dreams attend thee, maiden fair, good night!

Lis.   O holy Virgin, guard me thro' this night!

END OF THE FIRST ACT.

ACT II.

SCENE 1.—*The Village Street.*

CHORUS.

Weave the wreath and chant the lay,
As they wend upon their way;
See, the sun doth brightly shine,
Shedding forth his beams divine;—
List the minstrels' fifes and drums!
See, the gay procession comes!
Let our joyous shouts resound!
Hail our Queen with roses crown'd!

                [The procession enters.]
                [Dance.]

Pas.   To Heaven in gratitude I bow
That it has spared my life till now,
To gaze once more upon this scene,
And crown Lisette your village Queen.

BALLAD.

PASTOR.

I.

I have watched thee, gentle maiden,
   From thy childhood's earliest hour,
And seen with joy thy mind controll'd
   By virtue's holy power:
In this happy, humble village,
   Free from peril and from strife,
Thou hast known earth's greatest blessing—
   A pure and peaceful life.

II.

In thy childhood, thy dear parents
   From thy home were torn away,
And thou lost for ever, dear Lisette,
   Their guiding love and sway;
Yet thou from Virtue's pleasant ways
   Hast never turned aside,
In all thy actions thou hast made
   Her laws thy only guide.

Pas.   See! who comes here with hurried pace,
And signs of anger on her face?
Therian Tear the wreath from off her brow,
She's not worthy to be Queen!
Chorus Lisette not worthy!
Th.   No; not now!
List! I'll relate what I have seen,—
As late last night from work returning,
I saw a light in her chamber burning,
The shadow on the blind revealed
Some one was in her room concealed.
Cho.   Speak, speak, Lisette, can this be true?
Dare any one say this of you?
Great Heaven! with guilt she hangs her head,
The color from her cheeks has fled.

SOLO AND CHORUS.

LISETTE.

O fatal day! unhappy me!
What anguish and what misery
Must I endure for thy dear sake!
Alas, I feel my heart will break!

CHORUS.

O fatal day! unhappy maid!
Our trust in thee has been betray'd!
To think that form contains within
A heart that loves deceit and sin!

Pas.   Hence to thy home, base girl, begone!
           [Captain Antoine enters.]
Who is this stranger, pale and wan,
Who slowly drags his steps along,
Whose anxious gaze is on the throng?
Cap. A. Kind friends inform me if one Pierre,
The brother of Lisette, is here?

Pas.   No, Stranger, Pierre we have not seen:
This is Lisette, our village Queen.

TRIO.

CAPTAIN ANTOINE.

Lisette your Queen! and yet those eyes
So filled with tears, those deep-drawn sighs,
   Proclaim a heart but ill at rest;
(Aside) And was I base enough her name
   With words of slander to defame?
   I feel with shame and grief opprest!

PASTOR.

Why comes this stranger 'mongst us now
His falt'ring step and pallid brow
   Proclaim that wounded he has been;
What strange adventure brings him here?
Why does he seek the soldier Pierre?
   Why gaze thus on our village Queen?

LISETTE.

What stranger's this I gaze on now?
His falt'ring step and pallid brow
   Proclaim a sufferer is he:
But oh! my heart is chill'd with fear;
Why does he seek my brother Pierre?
   Why look so mournfully on me?

Cap. A. Why is your Queen in tears?
Pas.   We've found
She was not worthy to be crown'd.
Cap. A. I pray explain.
Pas.   With pain and grief
I tell the tale. Let me be brief,—
One of our neighbours has revealed
Some one was in her cot concealed—
Cap. A. Say when—
Pas.   The whole of yesternight.
Cap. A. Some one concealed! Ah! now a light
Upon me breaks.—Lisette, come near,
Tell me, sweet maiden, was it Pierre
You did conceal? Nay, do not fear,
For see, his pardon I have here.
Lis.   His pardon!
Cap. A.   Yes!
Lis.   Then he is free
From peril!
Cap. A.   You confess 'twas he!
Lis.   Alas, poor Pierre! he never more
   Will happiness regain,
But sorrow be his portion, for
   His Captain he has slain.

Cap. A. *(laughing.)* No, no, not slain! Lisette, in me
Pierre's captain and his friend you see.
Lis. and Chorus. Our seigneur's son!
          Captain Antoine!
Our noble seigneur's son!
Cap. A. Friends of my childhood, long I've been away,
But now with you henceforth I mean to stay.

CHORUS.

Welcome, welcome, our noble seigneur's son!
Honor and fame in the field he has won.
He leaves all the glories of war,
The sound of the trumpet afar,
The roll and the rattle of drums,
To the home of his childhood he comes.

Cap. A. Tell me, my friends, is not Lisette
Worthy to be your Queen?
Cho.   She is!
Cap. A.   Then let
The gay procession form again,
And peace and joy resume their reign.

FINALE.

LISETTE.

Now banish ev'ry fear,
   What happiness serene
Now fills my breast to bear
   I am their village Queen!

TUTTI.

Now wipe all tears away,
   Let nought but smiles be seen,
With heart and voice we say,
   Long live our village Queen.

INDEX.

THE ROSE OF SALENCY.

OVERTURE.

W. CHALMERS MASTERS.

Più allegro alla recitativo.

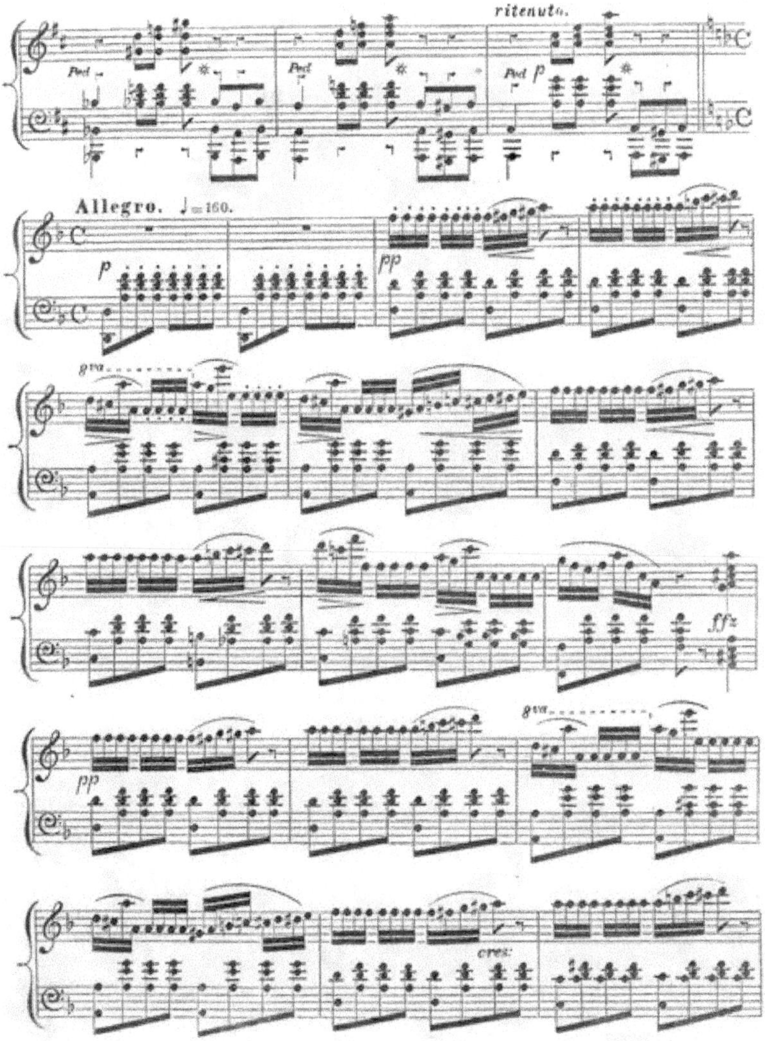
ritenuto.
Ped
Allegro. ♩= 160.
p
pp
8va
ffz
cres.

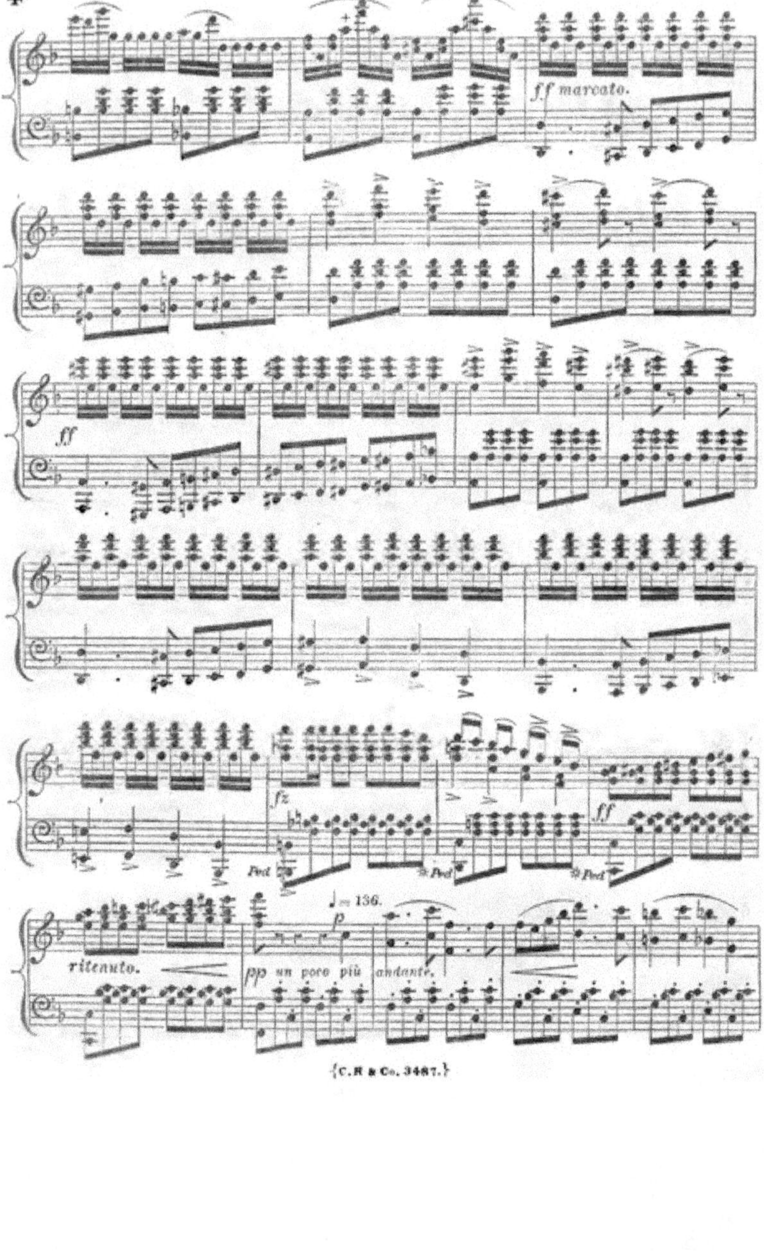
ff marcato.
ff
fz
Ped
ff
ritenuto.
♩= 136.
p
pp un poco più andante.

poco cres:
mf
cres: e
stringendo.
f
dim:
p e rall:
p
a tempo.
rall:
a tempo
p
cres: ed accel:
cres:
f
p
dim:

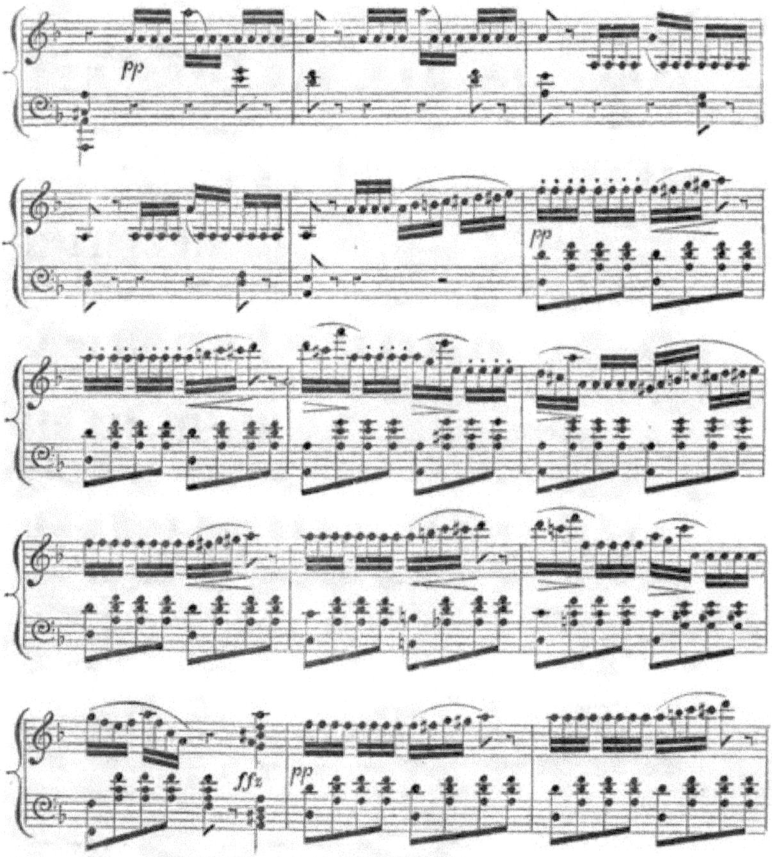
pp
pp
ffz
pp
8va
cres:

ff marcato.

ff

cres: ritenuto.   poco più andante.   p

(C.H & Co. 3487.)   LONDON: Printed by LAMBORN COCK, HUTCHINGS & Co., 63, New Bond Street.

SCENE I.

No 1. CHORUS.—"UPON THIS DAY."

WORDS & MUSIC BY
W CHALMERS MASTERS.

SOPRANO. Up.on this day we meet to choose A maiden

CONTRALTO. Up.on this day we meet to choose A maiden

TENOR. Up.on this day we meet to choose A maiden

BASS. Up.on this day we meet to choose A maiden

for our vil.lage Queen; On her a.lone our choice shall fall............ Whose life has

for our vil.lage Queen; On her a.lone our choice shall fall............ Whose life has

for our vil.lage Queen; On her a.lone our choice shall fall

for our vil.lage Queen; On her a.lone our choice shall fall

pure and spotless been.......... Nor wit nor beau.ty shall de.cide,

pure and spotless been.......... Nor wit nor beau.ty

Whose life has pure and spotless been. Nor

Whose life has pure and spotless been.

pp leggiero.

shall decide, But vir........tue be..........., vir......tue

wit nor beauty shall decide, But vir.....tue be, But vir...tue

Nor wit nor beauty shall de......cide, vir...tue

be........... vir........tue be our on.....ly guide. Nor

be But vir.....tue be our on.....ly guide. Nor

be........... But vir..........tue be our on.....ly guide. Nor

be vir.....tue be our on.....ly guide. Nor

wit nor beau..ty shall de..cide, But vir..tue be our on...ly guide, But

wit nor beau..ty shall de..cide, But vir..tue be our on...ly guide, But

wit nor beau..ty shall de..cide, But vir..tue be our on...ly guide, But

wit nor beau..ty shall de..cide, But vir..tue be our on...ly guide, But

vir..tue be our on..ly guide, our on...ly guide, our on.........ly

vir..tue be our on..ly guide, our on...ly guide, our on.........ly

vir..tue be our on..ly guide, our on...ly guide, our on.........ly

vir..tue be our on..ly guide, our on...ly guide, our on.........ly

guide, our on.........ly guide.

guide, our on.........ly guide.

guide, our on.........ly guide.

guide, our on.........ly guide.

[C. H & Co. 3488.] LONDON: Printed by LAMBORN COCK, HUTCHINGS & Co, 63, New Bond Street.

No 2. RECIT & CHORUS.

PASTOR.

Moderato.

Now neighbours all, each in your

PIANO.

p tremolo.

turn, Pass by and place within this urn A

pa...per with the mai.den's name Whom you would

wish...... o'er you to reign, And 'till an.o.ther year comes

round To be your Queen with ro....ses crown'd.

(C. H & C. 3185.)

CHORUS.—"NOW HOPE AND FEAR!"

WORDS & MUSIC BY
W. CHALMERS MASTERS.

Now hope and fear are striv......ing In many a mai..den's breast, But soon their fate de..cid..ing Each doubt will be at rest.

15

N.º 3. RECIT: & CHORUS.

WORDS & MUSIC BY
W. CHALMERS MASTERS.

PASTOR.

My friends with pleasure I an..nounce to all

PIANO.

Up..on Li.sette your choice doth fall.

CHORUS.—"HAPPY LISETTE."

Allegro con brio.
♩. = 100.

f brillante.

SOPRANO.

Happy Lisette re...joice.....! On thee hath fall'n our choice..... And

CONTR' ALTO.

re...joice.....! On thee hath fall'n our choice.....

TENOR.

re...joice.....! On thee hath fall'n our choice.....

BASS.

re...joice.....! On thee hath fall'n our choice.....

cres:
hap.py are we to gain............ Such a Queen o'er us to reign............ And
And hap.py are we to gain And hap.py are we to
And hap.py are we to gain And hap.py are we to
And hap.......py are we, are we to.........
p
cres:
f
p e legato.
happy are we to gain Such a Queen o'er us to reign. Thy
gain Such a Queen o'er us to reign. Thy
gain Such a Queen o'er us to reign.
gain Such a Queen o'er us to reign.
ff
(The same movement.)
pure and spot.less mind, Thy beau.ty and truth com..bin'd......... Will
pure and spot.less mind, Thy beau.ty and truth com..bind......... Will
(The same movement.)
8va
pp
delicato.

make us all hail the day When we bow to thy gen..tle

make us all hail the day When we bow to thy gen..tle

sway. Happy Lisette!

sway. Happy Lisette!

p con espress: Thy pure and spot..less mind, Thy

Thy pure and spot..less mind,

Happy Lisette!

Happy Lisette!

beau...ty and truth com....bin'd, Will make us all hail the

Thy beau...ty and truth combin'd, Will make us all hail the

{C. H & Co. 3480.}

Hap.py Li.sette re.
Hap.py Li.sette re.
day...... When we bow to thy gen..tle sway.
day...... When we bow to thy gen..tle sway.
-joice! Hap.py Li.sette re..joice! re..joice! re.
-joice! Hap.py Li.sette re..joice! re..joice! re.
ffz
ffz
ffz
-joice! Happy Lisette re.
-joice! re.
re.
re.
ff
ff
ff
ff
f brillante.
ff

_joice......! On thee hath fall'n our choice........ And hap-py are we to

_joice......! On thee hath fall'n our choice......... And

_joice...! On thee hath fall'n our choice......... And

_joice......! On thee hath fall'n our choice......... And

gain.......... Such a Queen o'er us to reign............. And hap-py are we to

hap-py are we to gain And hap-py are we to gain Such a

hap-py are we to gain And hap-py are we to gain Such a

hap..........py are we, are we to......... gain Such a

_gain Such a Queen o'er us to reign. Hap-py Li-sette! Hap-py Li-

Queen o'er us to reign. Hap-py Li-sette! Hap-py Li-

Queen o'er us to reign. Hap-py Li-

Queen o'er us to reign. Hap-py Li-

Segue Song Soprano.

N.º 4. SONG.

"I SHALL BE QUEEN OF ROSES."

WORDS & MUSIC BY
W. CHALMERS MASTERS.

{C. H & Co. 3491.}

bliss to...... feel that on my brow The beauteous wreath re...

_pos..........es! What tran_sport my dear friends to meet,

Each cheek with pleasure glow.......ing— And all a...... smile and

wel_come kind Up_on their Queen be_stow..........ing.

{c. 11 & c., 3491.}

I shall be Queen of

Ro...... ses! What bliss to...... feel that on my brow The

beau_teous wreath re....po.........ses!

When

lads and lass_es, gai....ly dress'd, Are on the green sward

dan......cing, And from each mai_den's spark_ling eye Pure

hap...pi...ness is glan........cing When Mu_sic's notes float

in the air, Mine ear with wel_come greet......ing, Be_

con espress:

_lieve me, friends, this heart will then With gra_ti__tude__be

beat_____ing.

I shall be Queen of Ro_____ses! What bliss to_____feel that

on my brow The beau_teous wreath re___po_____ses!

Nº 5. RECIT & CHORUS.

PASTOR

Moderato espressivo

church to-mor-row we will meet.

Each one drest   All in his best,   And there our future

più andante e sostenuto.

Queen we'll greet, Then 'neath the sa-cred dome we'll pray That

più andante e sostenuto.

Adagio.

heav'n will guide her on her way, And shield her from all care and

Adagio.

Tempo Iᵐᵒ

sor..........row.   So now good night un-til tomorrow.

Tempo Iᵐᵒ

{C. H & Co. 3492.}

CHORUS.—"TILL THE SUN."

WORDS & MUSIC BY
W. CHALMERS MASTERS.

Till the sun the o rient sky Is tint ing with golden ray, And nature wakes re joic ing To welcome a no ther day, Till the

sun the o - rient sky Is tint - ing with gol - den ray, And
sun the o - rient sky Is tint - ing with gol - den ray, And
sun the o - rient sky Is tint - ing with gol - den ray, And
sun the o - rient sky Is tint - ing with gol - den ray, And
na - ture wakes re - joic - - ing To wel - come a - no - ther day:
na - ture wakes re - joic - - ing To wel - come a - no - ther day:
na - ture wakes re - joic - - ing To wel - come a - no - ther day:
na - ture wakes re - joic - - ing To wel - come a - no - ther day: Till
p
pp
p
Till
p
Till
p
Till
thro' the am - bient air Is heard the ma - tin bell
pp

cres: e rall:

thro' the ambient air...... Is heard the ma-tin bell...... *p* *a tempo.*

thro' the ambient air...... Is heard the ma-tin bell, Fare-well fair Queen of

thro' the ambient air...... Is heard the ma-tin bell, Fare-well, fare-

Is heard the ma-tin bell, Fare-well

cres: e rall: *pp* *a tempo.*

(LISETTE.) Fare-well dear friends and neigh....bours, Fare-well dear friends and

(CHORUS.) Fare-well fair Queen of Ro.....ses, Fare-well fair Queen of

Ro.........ses, fair Queen of Ro.....ses, Fare-well fair Queen of

-well fair Queen of Ro.............ses, Fare-well fair Queen of

fair Queen of Ro.....ses, Fare-well fair Queen of

cres:

neigh.....bours, Un....til the morn fare-well.........., Fare-well dear friends and

Ro.....ses, Gen-tle Li-sette, fare-well.........., Fare-well fair Queen of

Ro.....ses, Gen-tle Li-sette, fare-well, Fare-well fair Queen of

Ro.....ses, Gen-tle Li-sette, fare-well..........

Ro.....ses, Gen-tle Li-sette, fare-well,

pp *p* *pp*

LONDON: Printed by LAMBORN COCK,
HUTCHINGS & Co. 63. New Bond Street.

SCENE II.

Nº 6. RECIT.—"O THIS HAS BEEN A HAPPY DAY."

Allegro.

LISETTE.

p

poco cres:

f

O this has been a hap-py

day!   How kind   my neighbours were, that they   Should

f

ffz

p

{C. B & Co. 3493.}

choose the or-phan girl Li-sette   To   be their Queen of

più andante.

Roses.   Yet,   I   can-not help   a

p più andante.

feel.....ing of re-gret   That my dear bro-ther is not here to share my

Andante molto.

joy.   Now I'll to rest re-..-pair;

Andante molto.

PED   *

PED

rall:

But   first   I'll of-..fer   up   a   pray'r.

fz rall:

p

*

(C. M & Co. 3101.)

PRAYER.—"O HOLY VIRGIN."

WORDS & MUSIC BY
W. CHALMERS MASTERS.

♩=120. Andante religioso.

una corda sempre.

O ho......ly Vir......gin guard......Thy ser......vant thro' the night......And

{C. H & Cº. 3493.}

o'er her slum.........bers watch.......................... Un.......
PED
.til the morn.......ing light.............................. And
pp
o'er her slum.........bers watch.......................... Un.
ppp
rall:
a tempo.
.til the morn.......ing light...... ......

poco cres: dim:

While

dark........ness shrouds the earth.............. From

dan..........ger keep me free........................, And

{C.R & Cᵒ. 4493.}

in   the morn   I'll sing............   Glad

prais.........es...... un.........to   thee   And

in   the morn   I'll sing.................   Glad

prais.........es   un.............to   thee........

{C. H & Co. 5493.}   LONDON: Printed by LAMBORN COCK, HUTCHINGS & Co, 64, New Bond Street.

Nº 7. RECIT. — "WHAT STEP IS THAT?"

LISETTE. What step is that? Who comes this way? My brother

PIERRE. Pierre! Hush! silence pray! Are we a-lone? Is no one near?

LISETTE. We are a-lone, but why this fear? Why on thy face that look forlorn, Thy dress all travel — stain'd and torn? What means all this?

PIERRE. My tongue will fail. To tell thee all the dreadful tale.

{C. H & Cº. 3494.}

Nº 7.

BALLAD _ "THE COTTAGE FAR AWAY."

WORDS & MUSIC BY
W. CHALMERS MASTERS.

40

know'st that I was forced to leave This hap_py, hum_ble

pp

cres:

f

cot   To   join   the   bu_sy,   tent__ed field, And

cres:

f

share   a sol_dier's   lot.   But 'midst   the din and clang of

dim: *mf*   *cres:*

arms,   In   bat...tle's fierce ar....ray,   I

f

dim: e rall:

(C. H & Co. 3404.)

thought of thee, my sis...ter dear, And the cot..tage far a...

pp a tempo.

con espress. rall:

...way ___ I thought of thee, my sis...ter dear, And the

rall:

cottage far.... a...way.

col voce. p a tempo.

p

At

night I paced the sen_try's round To guard a_gainst sur-
-prise, I gazed upon the star_ry heav'ns, And
thought of thy bright eyes. 'Midst
all the scenes of war and strife, For

one thing did I pray, Once more to see my

sis_ter dear, And the cot_tage far a....way__ Once

more to see my sis...ter dear, And the cottage far.. a_

..way.

44

No 8. RECIT & DUET.

WORDS & MUSIC BY
W. CHALMERS MASTERS.

LISETTE

Keep me no longer in sus–pense, dear Pierre, Tell me what

dire mis–for–tune brings you here.

PIERRE. *p tempo marziale.*

Thou know'st, Li–sette, our

♩ = 136. p tempo marziale ma andante.

Seigneur's son By valiant deeds has ho–nor won, But tho' a sol–dier

brave is he, He laughs at wo–man's pu–ri–ty. One day he dared to

cres molto.

...in thy name With words of in–fa–my and shame, En–rag'd I struck him.

cres: molto.

tremolo.

{C. H & Co. 3495.}

agitato
accel.
swords we drew— We fought— a-las! my sword plung'd thro' His
col voce.
accel.
Tempo Imo
side! he fell, and lay as dead; Struck with re-morse and fear I
ffz
p
Tempo Imo
p
fled..., For days and nights I wan-der'd on..., 'Till
p
più andante.
tired and worn, all hope near gone, I reach'd, at last this much-lov'd
pp più andante.
pp
home. Should I be found, death is my doom.
pp

DUET – "AS WHEN THE THREAT'NING THUNDER-CLOUD."

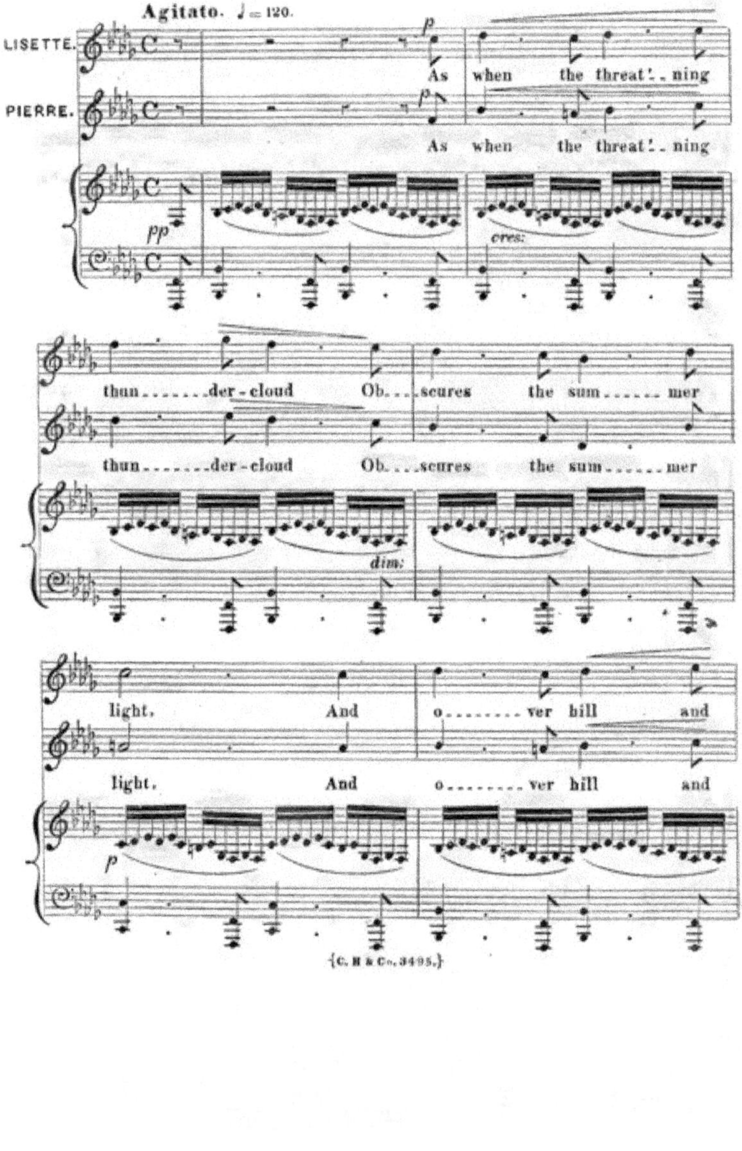

val.........ley casts A sha.......dow as of
val.........ley casts A sha.......dow as of
night: So
night: So now I feel that
p
p
now I feel that
cres: sempre.
sor.......row's blight Has fall'n up..on the
cres:

cres sempre.

sor..... row's blight   Has

scene,   And   grief   u - surps   the

fall'n,   has fall'n   up...on   the

place   where once   Reign'd hap.......pi - ness   su -

cres:

scene—   And   grief   u - surps   the

-preme—   And   grief   u - surps   the

{C. H & Co. 3495.} LONDON: Printed by LAMBORN COCK, HUTCHINGS & Co. 63, New Bond Street.

Nº 9. RECIT. & SERENADE.

Andante.

LISETTE.

Hark! I hear footsteps in the

street, The neighbours near my win..dow

accel:

meet, Quick! to my bedroom, Take this

rall:

light, All an..gels guard thee Pierre! Good night!

Nº 9. SERENADE.—SWEET DREAMS ATTEND.

WORDS & MUSIC BY
W. CHALMERS MASTERS.

♩=104. **Andante non troppo lento.**

SOPRANO.
Sweet dreams at.tend thy sleeping Mai.den fair, All an . gels o'er thee
keep...ing Watch.ful care, Un..til the lark is sing............ing His
ma...........tin lay..., And village bells are ring...ing In the day.

CONTRALTO.
Sweet dreams at.tend thy sleeping Mai.den fair, All an . gels o'er thee
keep.....ing Watch.ful care, Un..til the lark is sing...........ing His
ma............tin lay..., And village bells are ringing In the day. And

TENOR.
Sweet dreams at.tend thy sleeping Mai.den fair, All an . gels o'er thee
keep...ing Watch.ful care, Un..til the lark is
sing.ing His matin lay, And village bells are ring...ing In the day.

BASS.
Sweet dreams at tend thy sleeping Mai.den fair, All an . gels o'er thee
keep...ing Watch.ful care, Un..til the lark is
sing.ing His matin lay, And village bells are ring..ing In the day.

ACCOMPT:
ad lib.

(C. H & Co. 3496.)

And vil.lage bells are ring ing In the day. Sweet dreams....

vil.lage bells are ring....ing In the.... day. Sweet

are ring.....ing In the day.

And vil.lage bells are ring.ing In the day.

Sweet dreams at.tend thy sleep..ing

dreams......... Sweet dreams at.tend thy sleep..ing

Sweet dreams......... Sweet dreams at.tend thy sleep..ing

Sweet dreams, Sweet dreams at.tend thy sleep..ing

Mai...den fair, All an..gels o'er thee keep..ing Watch.ful

Mai...den fair, All an..gels o'er thee keep.......ing Watch.ful

Mai...den fair, All an..gels o'er thee keep..ing Watch.ful

Mai...den fair, All an.gels o'er thee keep.....ing Watch.ful

LONDON: Printed by LAMBORN COCK, HUTCHINGS & Co. 63 New Bond Street.
{C.H & Co. 3496.}

End of Act I.

ACT II.

Nº 10. CHORUS — "WEAVE THE WREATH."

WORDS & MUSIC BY
W. CHALMERS MASTERS.

SOPRANO.
chant the lay, ... chant the

CONTRALTO.
chant the lay, ... chant the

TENOR.
Weave the wreath, ... Weave the wreath,

BASS.
Weave the wreath, ... Weave the wreath,

lay, Weave the wreath and chant the lay, As they wend up..on their

lay, Weave the wreath and chant the lay, As they wend up..on their

Weave the wreath and chant the lay, As they wend up..on their

Weave the wreath and chant the lay, As they wend up..on their

way, Weave the wreath and chant the lay, As they wend up.on their way.
way, Weave the wreath and chant the lay, As they wend up.on their way.
way, Weave the wreath and chant the lay, As they wend up.on their way.
way, Weave the wreath and chant the lay, As they wend up.on their way.
p
p
See, the sun doth brightly shine....,
p
Shedding forth his beams di...
pp delicato.
..vine......
ff
List the minstrels' fifes and drums..!
ff
List the minstrels' fifes and drums!
ff
List the minstrels' fifes and drums..!
ff
List the minstrels' fifes and drums..!
f

56

See the gay pro-ces-sion comes! List the minstrels' fifes and

See the gay pro-ces-sion comes! List the minstrels' fifes and

See the gay pro-ces-sion comes! List the minstrels' fifes and

See the gay pro-ces-sion comes!

drums! See the gay pro-ces-sion comes!

drums! See the gay pro-ces-sion comes!

drums! See the gay pro-ces-sion comes!

List the minstrels' fifes and drums! See the gay pro-ces-sion

See the gay pro ces sion comes!

See the gay pro ces sion comes!

See the gay pro ces sion comes!

comes! the gay pro ces sion comes!

f brillante.

Weave the
Weave the
Weave the
Weave the

wreath and chant the lay, As they wend up_on their way; Let our
wreath and chant the lay, As they wend up_on their way; Let our
wreath and chant the lay, As they wend up_on their way; Let our
wreath and chant the lay, As they wend up_on their way; Let our

joy......ous shouts re...sound! Hail our Queen with ro_ses crown'd! Let our
joy......ous shouts re...sound! Hail our Queen with ro_ses crown'd! Let our
joy......ous shouts re...sound! Hail our Queen with ro_ses crown'd! Let our
joy......ous shouts re...sound! Hail our Queen with ro_ses crown'd! Let our

{C. H & Co. 1497.}

58

{C. H & Co. 3497.}

{C. H & Co. 3497.} LONDON: Printed by LAMBORN COCK, HUTCHINGS & Co., 63, New Bond Street.

Nº 11.

VILLAGERS' DANCE.

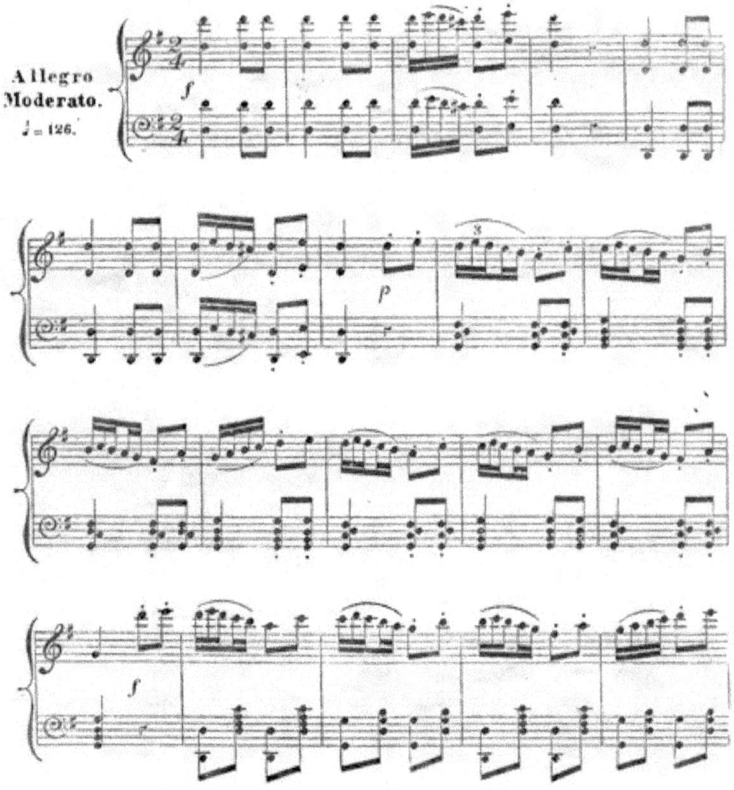
Allegro
Moderato.
♩ = 126.
f
p
3
f

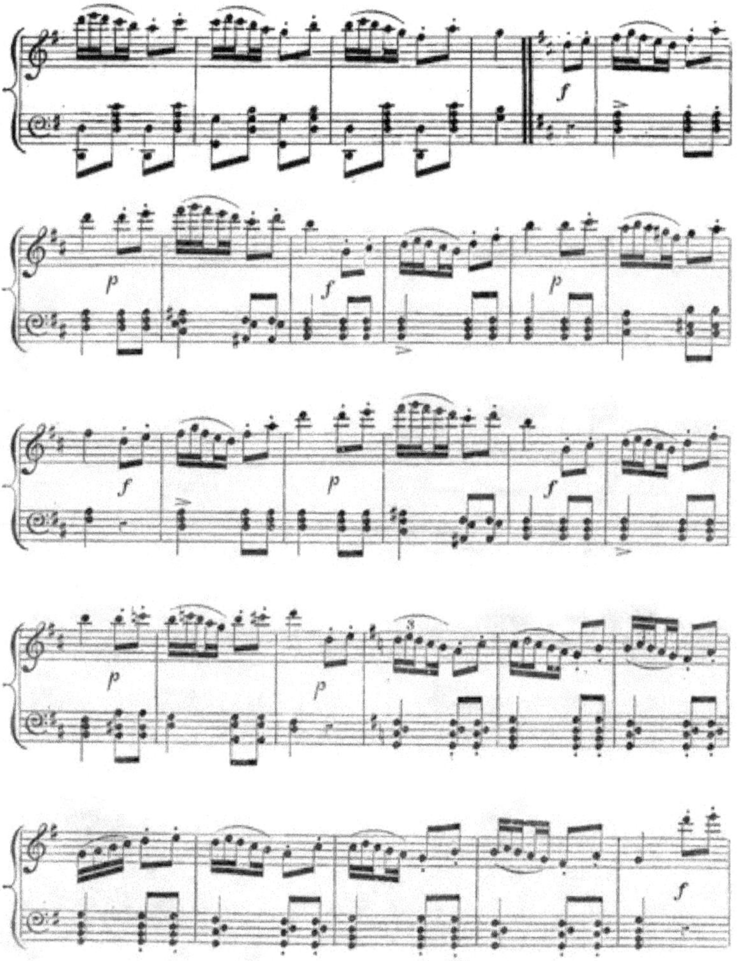

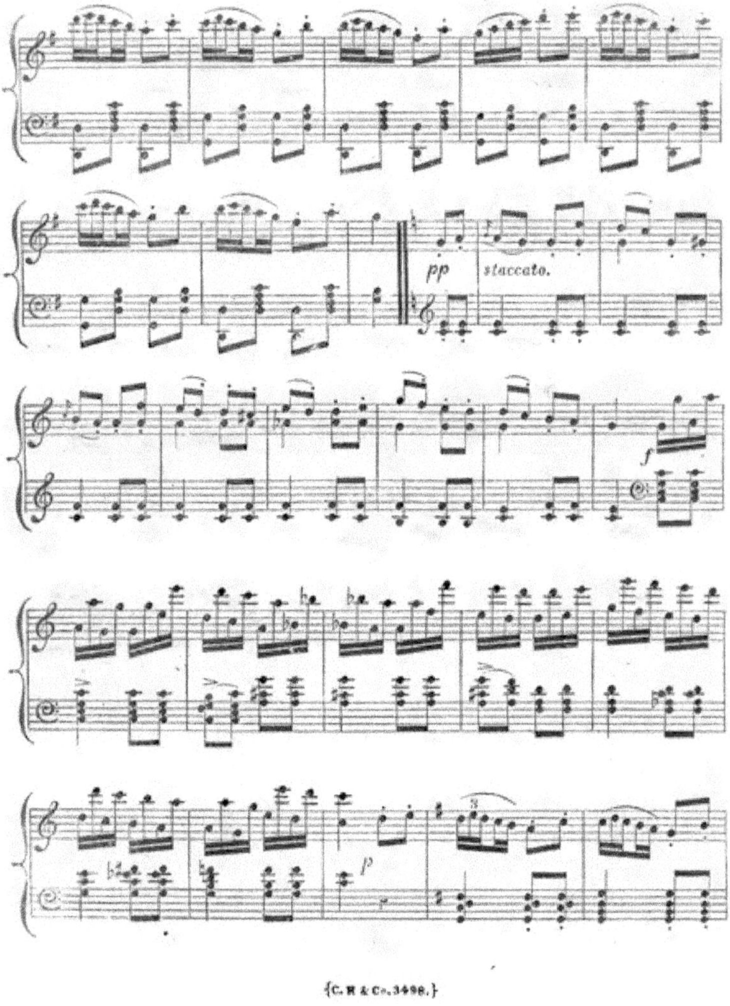
pp
staccato.
f
p

{C. M & Co. 3498.}   LONDON: Printed by LAMBORN COCK, HUTCHINGS & Co, 63, New Bond Street.

PED

Nº 12. RECIT. & BALLAD.

Andante. ♩ = 112.

PASTOR.

To

Heav'n in gra_titude I bow   That it has spared my life 'till

now,   To gaze once more up_on this scene,

And crown Li_sette your vil_lage Queen.

BALLAD—"I HAVE WATCHED THEE, GENTLE MAIDEN."

WORDS & MUSIC BY
W. CHALMERS MASTERS.

I have watch'd thee, gen _ tle maiden, From thy

childhood's ear_liest hour, And seen with joy thy

mind con_troll'd By virtue's ho_ly pow'r: In this hap_py, humble

vil_lage, Free from pe_ril and from strife, Thou hast

known earth's greatest blessing, Thou hast known earth's greatest

bles_ _ sing A pure and peace_ _ful life.

{C. B & C. 3499.}

In thy childhood thy dear pa_rents From thy home were torn a__way, And thou lost for e_ver, dear Li_sette, Their gui__ding love and sway; Yet thou from Vir_tue's

{C. H & C_, 3499.}

pleasant ways Hast ne_ver turn'd a.....side,   In

all thy ac_tions thou hast made Her laws thy on..ly

guide...... Her laws thy on.....ly guide.

No 13. RECIT & SOLO—"Tear the wreath from off her brow."

Allegro molto ed agitato.

PASTOR. See! who comes here with har...ried pace, And signs of an......ger on her face?

THÉRÈSE. Tear the wreath from off her brow, She's not wor.....thy to be Queen! No, not now! List I'll re.late what I have seen—

SOPR. Lisette not worthy!
CONTR. Lisette not worthy!
TENOR. Lisette not worthy!
BASS. Lisette not worthy!

{C. H & Co. 3500.}

70

Moderato. ♩ = 120.

As late last night from work re‥turn‥ing, I

saw a light in her cham‥ber burn‥ing, The sha‥dow on the

blind re‥veal'd A man was in her room con‥ceal'd!

CHORUS.

Speak, speak Lisette, can this be true? Dare a‥ny one say

Speak, speak Lisette, can this be true? Dare a‥ny one say

Speak, speak Lisette, can this be true? Dare a‥ny one say

Speak, speak Lisette, can this be true? Dare a‥ny one say

this of you? Great Heav'n! with guilt she hangs her head, Great
this of you? Great Heav'n! with guilt she hangs her head, Great
this of you? Great Heav'n! with guilt she hangs her head, Great
this of you? Great Heav'n! with guilt she hangs her head, Great
molto.
ff dim. p
Heav'n! with guilt she hangs her head, The co....... lor
Heav'n! with guilt she hangs her head, The co....... lor
Heav'n! with guilt she hangs her head, The co....... lor
Heav'n! with guilt she hangs her head, The co....... lor
ff dim. p
p
dim.
from her cheeks has fled.
from her cheeks has fled.
from her cheeks has fled.
from her cheeks has fled.
dim.

SOLO & CHORUS — "O FATAL DAY."

WORDS & MUSIC BY
W. CHALMERS MASTERS.

Andante molto. ♩= 66.

L. SETTE

O fa..tal day! un..hap..py me! What an..guish

and what mi..se...ry Must I en..dure for thy dear

sake! A..las, I feel my heart will break! O fa..tal

day! un..hap..py me....! What an..guish and what mi..se..

SOPRANO. O fa..tal day! un..hap..py

CONTRALTO. O fa..tal day! un..hap..py

TENOR. O fa..tal day! un..hap..py

BASS. O fa..tal day! un..hap..py

Soprano/Tenor: -ry... Must I en_dure for thy dear sake! Alas! I feel my heart will

Voices: maid! O fa_tal day! un_hap.........py

break! O fatal day! unhap_py me! What anguish and what mi_se_

maid! O fa_tal day! unhap_py maid! Our trust in thee has been be_

-ry... Must I en_dure for thy dear

_tray'd! To think that form contains with_in...

{C.H & Co. 3500.} LONDON: Printed by LAMBORN COCK, HUTCHINGS & Co. 64, New Bond Street.

Nº 14. RECIT & TRIO.

Andante.

PASTOR.

Hence to thy home base girl, be....gone!

Who is this stranger, pale and wan, Who slow..ly drags his

steps a...long, Whose an..xious gaze is on the throng?

CAPTAIN ANTOINE.

Kind friends inform me if one Pierre, The brother of Lisette is here?

PASTOR. Moderato.

No, Stranger, Pierre we have not seen: This is Li-sette, our vil-lage Queen.

f sostenuto.

WORDS & MUSIC BY
W. CHALMERS MASTERS.

Andante Espressivo. ♩ = 96.

CAPTAIN ANTOINE.

Li......sette   your

Queen!   and   yet   those   eyes   So   fill'd   with

tears,   those   deep — drawn   sighs,   Pro......claim   a

p (aside)

heart   but   ill   at   rest;   And   was ..   I

{C. H & Co. 3501.}

cres:
base e.......nough her name With words of
slan......der to de......fame? I feel with
grief and shame op..prest!
col voce.
dim:
p
PASTOR.
p
Li..... sette... your
Why comes this stran.......ger 'mongst us
cres.................
Queen! and yet.... those
now? His fal.......t'ring step and pal......lid

sighs Pro.....claim a heart but ill at

brow Pro.....claim that wound.......ed he has

rest.

been; What strange ad.....ven.........ture brings... him

A.....las! A...

here? Why does... he seek the sol.......dier

_las! I feel with grief and shame op-

Pierre? Why gaze thus on our vil.....lage

rall:

(C. H & C...1501.)

-prest!
Queen?
cres:
dim:
pp
PED
LISETTE.
p
What stran.... ger's this I gaze on now? His
Li.... sette your Queen!
What stran.... ger's this?
fal.... t'ring step and pal.......lid brow Pro... claim a
and yet those sighs Pro..
Why comes he here? Why
cres:
suf......fer....er is he: But oh! my heart is
-claim a heart but ill at rest.
comes he here?

chill'd with fear! Why does he seek my bro...ther Pierre? Why

A....las! A....las! I

What stran..ger's this? What brings him here? Why

look so mourn..ful...ly... on me? Why does he seek my

feel with grief and shame op..prest! I feel with grief and

does he seek the sol....dier Pierre? What strange ad...ven...ture

bro...ther Pierre? Why look thus mourn..ful..ly on me?

shame op..prest! I feel with grief and shame op..prest!

brings him here? Why does he seek the sol..dier Pierre?

     LONDON: Printed by LAMBORN COCK, HUTCHINGS & Co, 63, New Bond Street.

No 15. RECIT & CHORUS.

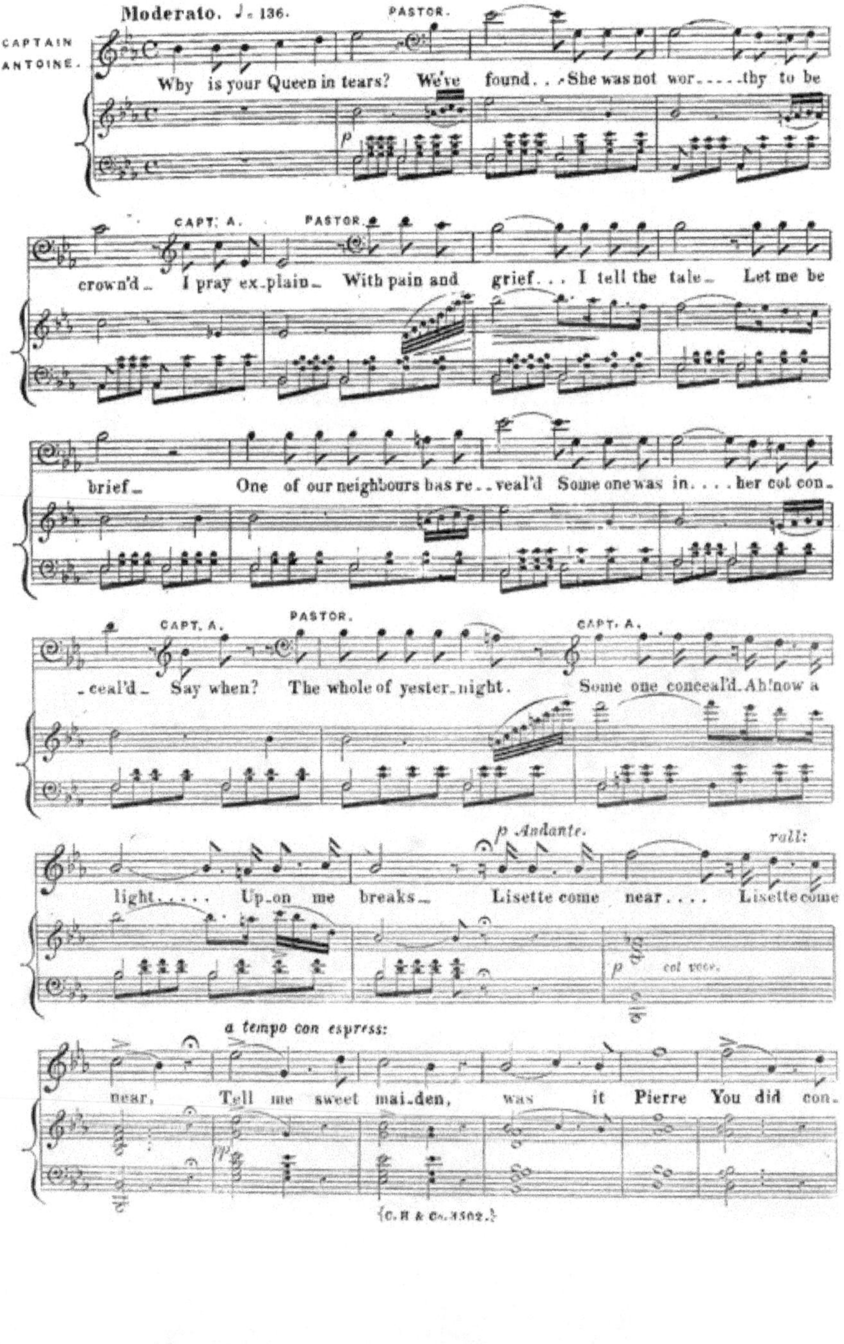

ceal? Nay do not fear, For see his par_don I have

here, For see.. his par_don I... have here. His pardon!

CAPT: A. **LISETTE.** **CAPT: A.** **LISETTE.**

Yes! Then he is free! His par_don! Yes! Then he is

CAPT: A. *rall:* **Andante.** ♩=96 **LISETTE.**

free from pe_ril! You confess 'twas he! A..

_las poor Pierre! he ne_ver more Will hap_pi_ness re_gain, But

CAPT: A. *più allegro*

sor_row be his por_tion, for His Cap_tain he has slain. No!no!not

{C.H & Co. 3507.}

LISETTE.

slain! Lisette in me Pierre's captain and his friend you see! Our seigneur's

son,........! Captain An_toine......! Our no_ble seigneur's son!

SOPR.
Our seigneur's son! Captain Antoine! Our no_ble seigneur's son!

CONTR.
Our seigneur's son! Captain Antoine! Our no_ble seigneur's son!

TENOR.
Our seigneur's son! Captain Antoine! Our no_ble seigneur's son!

BASS.
Our seigneur's son! Captain Antoine! Our no_ble seigneur's son!

CAPTAIN ANTOINE.
Maestoso.

Friends of my child__hood, long I've been a___way,

But now with you hence__forth I mean to stay.

{C.B & Co. 3502.}

Nº 15. CHORUS. — "WELCOME OUR NOBLE SEIGNEUR'S SON."

WORDS & MUSIC BY
W. CHALMERS MASTERS.

Wel - come our seigneur's son!
Wel - come our seigneur's son!
son, our seigneur's son!
son, our seigneur's son!
f
Ho - nor and fame in the
f marcato.
f
Ho - nor and fame in the
f
Ho - nor and fame in the field he has won, has won.
f
Ho - nor and fame in the field he has won. Ho - nor and
field he has won, has won, in the field has won.
field he has won, in the field he has won.
Ho - - nor and fame in the field he has won.
fame in the field, in the field he has won.
in the field he has won.
cres.
ff

Ho_nor and fame in the field he has won, in the field he has

Ho_nor and fame in the field he has won, in the field he has

Ho _ nor and fame in the field, in the field he has

he has won Ho_nor and fame in the

won, has won, in the field he has won.

won, has won, in the field he has won.

won in the field he has won.

field he has won, in the field he has won.

Wel_come, Welcome, Welcome our noble seigneur's son!

Wel_come, Welcome, Welcome our noble seigneur's son!

Wel_come, Welcome, Wel........come, Wel_come our noble seigneur's

Wel_come, Welcome, Wel........come, Wel_come our noble seigneur's

Wel.come our no.ble seigneur's son, Wel.come our seigneur's
Wel.come our no.ble seigneur's son, Wel.come our seigneur's
son, our no...ble seigneur's son, our seigneur's
son, our no...ble seigneur's son, our seigneur's
son! He leaves all the glo...ries of
son! He leaves all the glo...ries of
son! He leaves all the glo..ries of war, The
son! He leaves all the glo..ries of war, The
p cres: Ped
war, The sound of the trum.pet a...far, The
war, The sound of the trum.pet a...far, The
sound of the trumpet a..far, The roll and the rat.tle of
sound of the trumpet a...far, The roll and the rat.tle of
cres:
fz p cres: fz Ped

cres:
roll and the rat_tle of drums, To the home of his childhood he
roll and the rat_tle of drums, To the home of his childhood he
drums, To the home of his childhood he comes, To the
drums, To the home of his childhood he comes, To the
cres:
cres:
comes, To the home of his child_hood he comes! To the
comes, To the home of his child_hood he comes! To the
home, To the home of his child_hood he comes! To the
home, To the home of his child_hood he comes! To the
home of his childhood he comes! Wel_come, Wel_come,
home of his childhood he comes! Wel_come, Wel_come,
home of his childhood he comes! Wel_come, Wel_come,
home of his childhood he comes! Wel_come, Wel_come.

Welcome our noble seigneur's son! Wel_come our noble seigneur's
Welcome our noble seigneur's son! Wel_come our noble seigneur's
Wel.........come, Welcome our noble seigneur's son! our
Wel.........come, Welcome our noble seigneur's son! our
son! Welcome our seigneur's son.........
son! Welcome our seigneur's son! Wel_come,
no...ble seigneur's son, our seigneur's son! Wel_come,
no...ble seigneur's son, our seigneur's son! Wel_come,
Wel_come, Wel_come our seigneur's son.........!
Wel_come, Wel_come our seigneur's son.........!
Wel_come, Wel_come our seigneur's son.........!
ff
Ped
tremolo

90

No 16. RECIT. — "TELL ME, MY FRIENDS."

Moderato.

{C. H & Co. 3503.}

No 16. FINALE.— "NOW BANISH EV'RY FEAR."

Tempo di Valse non troppo presto.
con eleganza.

WORDS & MUSIC BY
W. CHALMERS MASTERS.

LISETTE.

..Now ban..ish ev'..ry fear......., What happi....ness se.

..rene....... Now fills my breast to hear.......... I am their village Queen.......!

SOPRANO.
CONTRALTO.
TENOR.
BASS.

Now

wipe all tears a...way.............. Let nought but smiles be seen......., With heart and

{O. H & Co. 3503.}

p e staccato.
cres:
voice we say......................, Long live our vil....lage Queen..........
Now ban...ish ev'....ry fear, What hap...pi...ness se...rene Now fills my breast to hear I am, I am.... their vil....lage Queen..............!
pp
Long live our Queen! Long live our Queen.............. Long live our Queen..............!
ppp
pp
f

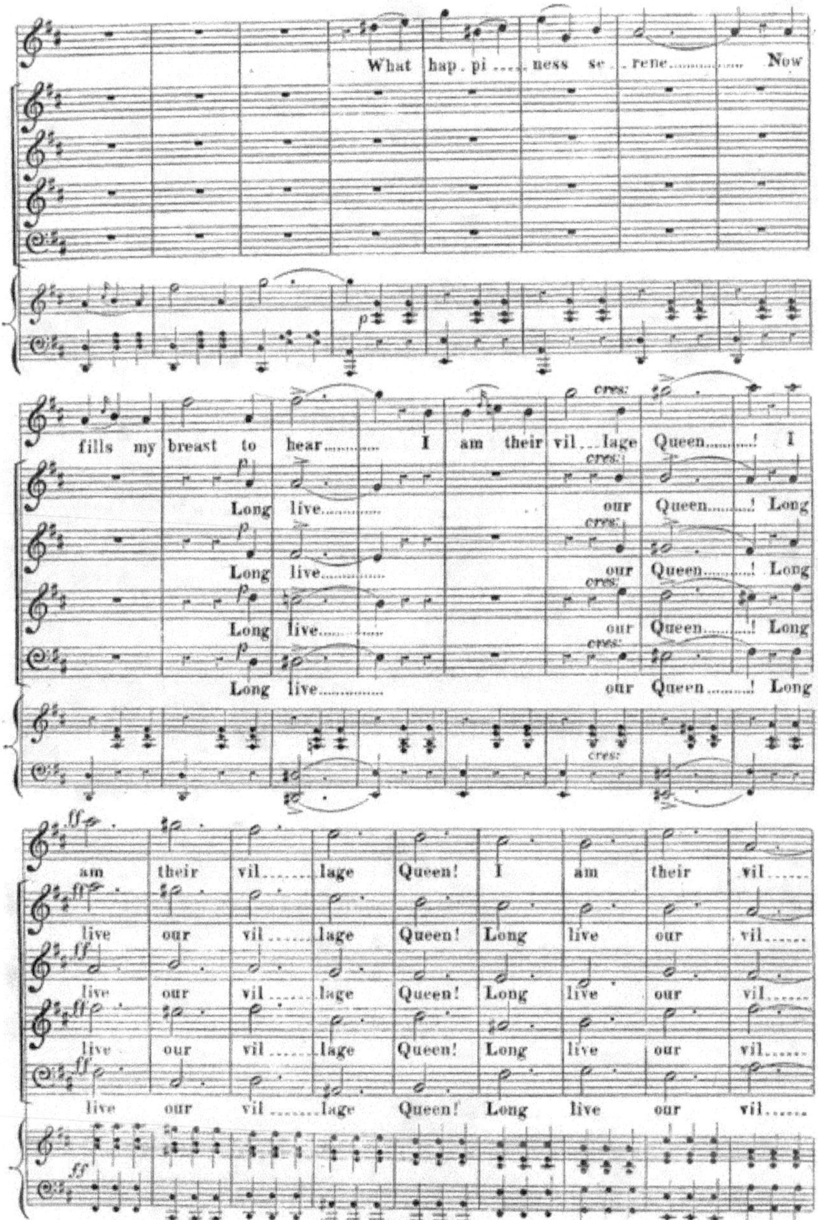

Printed by Lamborn Cock, Hutchings & Co. 63, New Bond Street.